The Gift Within

By Debbie Gumede

ISBN assigned: 978-0-620-64234-7

Acknowledgements

Special thanks to my husband Thobile who has always allowed me to do what makes me happy. When he asked me what I wanted to do with my life, I told him, amongst other things, that I wanted to write and he said, 'then write, what is stopping you?' I told him I did not have the inspiration, and he told me to create the environment. I thank him especially for his support while writing this book.

I also want to thank Paidamoyo Matongoti for taking the time to read the manuscript and giving me valuable input, which made this book a success. It was really encouraging to hear her say, 'Go girl!'

Many thanks to my uncle, Dominic Magwada, who is part of the inspiration somewhere in this book and who took the time to go through the manuscript and give valuable advice and input. He believed in Judah's journey, as he called it.

I also thank Pastor Brian Kuppusami. Pastor told me that if God has given us the grace to do something, then we must make use of it and capitalize on it.

A lot of people contribute to the publication of a book. Even though I may not be able to mention by name all who contributed to this book, I would like to express my sincere gratitude to you all, for making my dream a reality.

God bless you and may the gift within you continue to flourish.

We all have a gift within us.

Some are unwrapping their gift already and enjoying every moment of life.

Others are waiting to be told to start unwrapping their gift. Well, don't wait any longer start right now and discover the wonders inside.

Others are afraid to accept the gift because they are concerned about what people will say. It does not matter what people think, it is your gift so accept it and unwrap it.

Whatever your gift is – remember to cherish it and enjoy it every moment.

That my friends is the secret to living a fulfilled life.

It really does not matter how old you are, God intends for you to live a life full of colour, a life of beauty and a life of purpose.

Introduction

He put it in each and every one of us.

He placed it so deep within us, that it remains in us, waiting for us to connect with it and allow it to express itself through us. The amazing characteristic of the seed or gift God places inside us is its persistent knocking, until we express it.

People in every walk of life, around the globe, will relentlessly keep searching consciously or unconsciously for the missing link, until they connect with their gift.

When you hit the chord of your gifting it all makes sense. Something in you explodes because your gift has finally found its door to express itself, its entrance to beautifying the world.

Chapter One

Judah

For so many days now, Judah had stayed indoors, wondering what to do with his life. Ever since he had lost his one year job as a bookkeeper, Judah was losing zest for life. It was not as if he had been passionate about being a bookkeeper, but the job kept him busy. He was only motivated to work by the salary cheque at the end of the month, which was his livelihood. Like many people, he was caught up in the rut of life, where work is a means to an end not an expression of being who you are.

Despite his so many attempts to find another job, he had no prospects of success. It was now nine months and discouragement had nestled in his heart.

During this time at home, Judah found himself small jobs here and there, for a small fee, to keep him going. Although he was getting help from friends now and again, he knew that it was not life. He could not keep waiting for the next person to hand him something. He needed to do something for himself because failure to do so, would lead to nothing but poverty.

Judah was fully aware that everyone needs help somewhere along the line, but it was foolish to expect to be on the receiving-end forever. His mother had taught him that it was more blessed to give than to receive. There is no shame in receiving from others, but it was wrong to consciously be on the lookout for the next handout. While he never slept on an empty stomach, Judah could not afford buying essentials like fresh fruit when he had cash in his hands, neither could he afford the luxury of spoiling himself once in a while.

It was not possible for him to enjoy the pleasures of life as long as there was a price tag to it. Judah soon came to realize that in order to survive one needed the abundance of the God-given air all around and the generous donations from loved ones. However, in order to live, you needed to make it happen yourself. There is a huge difference between living and surviving and Judah had come to that realization the hard way.

Judah was an able young man, intelligent, handsome and healthy. He had an amicable personality and was humble. He was a relational fellow who could easily get along with anyone and seemed to make friends easily if he chose to. He was not talkative but neither was he a quiet guy. Judah was very speculative and his easy-going attitude made him likeable.

He wanted financial freedom. He wanted to become significant and not just successful. His wishes were far from being granted as long as he succumbed to the circumstances in his life that always rob him of the chance to get started. Judging by looks Judah could fit in with those people who had it easy in life, but his reality was different.

His family was neither rich nor poor and lived in the decent middle-class suburbs. When he compared himself to his fellow peers, Judah felt like a failure. He did not have a permanent decent job nor a house of his own (he lived in his parents' second house). He did not have a car, let alone any assets tied to his name. Unfortunately he frequently compared himself to others and usurped his self-esteem. He was not aware that it was self-defeating to live life through the lenses of other people.

Another factor that seemed to hinder Judah's breakthrough was that he did not have a life-coach. Maybe it was not a factor against him, because there was really no need for a mentor in his life, since he was not going anywhere. Without a specific purpose in life was there really a need for him to have a mentor?

They say in life when the student is ready the teacher appears[1]. For every successful man there is, it seems, that God-sent and God-prepared set man. It is almost a divine appointment, the way success links a person to the right person at the right time to make the transition from the ordinary life, to the extraordinary life. Judah was yet to encounter his set-man and at this stage in his life, he did not really expect to find such a man.

---

[1] Quote from Dr. Bob Butera

Chapter Two

Fueled to Action

*Despite the hidden potential buried in the seed, it is a biblical truth that unless a seed is planted and dies it can never be fruitful or multiply.*2

It is a normal summer day, but the only difference with today, is that Judah decides to plant the seeds that his mother had placed in his hands a long time ago. "Plant them," she had said, "and you will be amazed what a seed can do." Without wanting to hurt his mother's feelings, Judah had taken the seeds and kept them.

Today it suddenly dawned on him that the seeds would never produce anything amazing as long as they were stored in the cupboard. With that realization, he resolves to do something different which is also triggered by a desire to change the results he is getting in his life. The only task he can do immediately is clean out the garden, which is in a state. There are weeds everywhere. The garden is nothing, but a piece of idle neglected land that is a haven of weeds of every kind.

The weather is pleasant with a cool breeze that invitingly beads everyone to stay outdoors. Judah starts awkwardly pulling out the long weeds. Initially his clean fingers flick off the dirt as he pulls each weed from the ground. It does not take long for his right hand to get dirty and the dirt does not bother him anymore.

Judah works diligently, squeezing out the hard clumped soil. He feels the tenderness of the soil between his fingers as he works. He toys with the soil, feeling its texture. He breathes deeply as the rich smell of crude earth wades up his nostrils. This thrills him and awakens his soul. He has not experienced this inner joy for such a long time.

Even though he has not completely connected with the soil at this moment, there is definitely some chemistry happening between him and the soil. Judah has no intentions of becoming a farmer, but, contrary to that thought, the dirty hands bring him satisfaction. There's a smile on his face as he tries to rub off the dirt from his hands but he decides to continue with the task at hand.

The chore was laborious at the beginning but before he knows it, the day is spent and the task is done.

When you are doing something purposeful that brings with it fulfillment, time ticks by so fast. Even if time was to slow down, it would not bother you, because ultimately it would still take you to that place of accomplishment.

Judah stands amazed as he looks with pride at the garden. He is tired, very tired and sweaty yet at the same time he feels very content. Today he has accomplished something only he can be proud of.

Judah remains staring at the garden as if counting the clumps of soil he had turned over throughout the day. He is lost in his thoughts. Judah then takes a deep breath and breathes out. He is happy.

Was it not written that God would bless the labours of his hands[3]? That's what his mother always said but he had not actually seen where it was written. It was probably from the bible, the book his mother read daily without fail, yet a book he did not have time for, nor had he come to understand why his mother had treasured it so much.

It excites Judah a little to remember that promise from the word of God, but his inner voice reminds himself not to get too excited. In the past he had worked with his hands so many other times and had never seen the blessing overflow. Judah is skeptical about spiritualizing this whole garden experience. He has only cleared the garden and not planted a vineyard.

He wonders for a while about this religious saying that the labours of his hands are blessed. He does not believe in it and why should he? The joy he was feeling disappears. Even if he was religious, there is no way he could just become blessed because he did some digging.

Judah shrugs off the thoughts. If his success is not coming as a blessing, then his success was going to come through hard work. He was going to focus his time and effort on this garden until it gave him the results he wanted.

Chapter Three

The Decision

A little effort and doing something about it, had transformed a neglected garden, only in a day's work.

The future had so much in store for Judah, but it was really up to him to design and colour the future he wanted for himself. Judah is no mundane kind of person. He wants a colourful life and he realizes that he is the architect and artist of that life.

Sitting in the silence of his room, he remembers a book that he had read a couple of months back. What was the book again? It was titled "First Step", yes, that was the book.

He shakes his head almost in self-condemnation at the realization that it has taken him so many months to take his first step. He muses over it and tells himself, "Well, at least I have taken the first step now". The words come out loud than he expected and they give him the comfort is seeking. The book had expounded on the fact that nothing ever starts without the first step. To build a mansion you need to lay the first brick. To count to a million you need to start at one. It all adds up and builds up, but it all starts with the first step. Every success starts by taking the first step. When he had read it, it sounded so simple but execution of the first step for him had taken months. As long as he never put the effort to start, Judah's life was not going anywhere. As long as he stayed seated on his laurels, the first step did not automatically happen. It was his action, his effort that made the first step happen.

Judah celebrates this first step as his first success. He decides that he would build on it one day at a time, small actions at a time and see where it will take him. He has a sketchy idea of where he wants to go but the vision was still blurred. As he lies on his bed with his eyes closed, Judah paints the picture of his expectations in his mind. It feels good to dream and it all seems to be within his reach.

The second step for Judah was to plant the seeds. Judah makes a decision before he sleeps. Tomorrow he was definitely going to plant those seeds.

Chapter Four

What if...?

The new day dawns upon Judah with new energy, but as he pulls himself out of bed, his body aches from yesterday's work. Yesterday, due to the manual work he had done, he had exercised muscles he had never used before. Despite the pain, he stretches himself and while his body and mind attempt to psyche him that maybe this gardening is not such a good idea, his heart hums a different tune. His heart is for the garden, the dirty hands, the smell of the soil and the labour, but his body wants to rest and do nothing or maybe, just take it easy.

While stretching himself his eyes catch sight of the packet of seeds he had put on his dresser.

A packet of spinach seeds!

Spinach...!

How many people eat spinach?

What will he do with the spinach?

Sell it – but where?

Could he sell to the large vegetable market?

Not really- because they probably grow their own on hectares of land.

Could he sell it in his neighbourhood?

Maybe- but how many people in his neighbourhood ate spinach?

As the questions come and bombard his mind one after the other, Judah finds himself sitting on his bed no longer as enthusiastic about the garden as when he had opened his eyes. Something about these questions dampened his spirits. He lingers in the room for a while then he realizes that as long as he stays in that room, the dream will never become his reality. The atmosphere in the room has nothing to offer in order to rejuvenate yesterday's excitement. He needs to get out and get out fast. In a state of rush, he fumbles his shoes on and makes his way towards the door that leads him to the garden. He can hardly wait to get out of the house.

As he pulls the door open towards himself, the morning breeze splashes itself against Judah's face. The morning fresh air embraces itself all over his skin, which is not covered by his pajamas and aerates itself to the rest of his body. It feels sensational. It awakens his being. He is wide awake now, he is alive. This is life, not the somber life he had just experienced minutes earlier in his room.

All his cares evaporate as he steps outside. It is as if he is stepping into a new world he has never been in before. This morning is probably like yesterday's morning, but yesterday he did not come outside this early. Yesterday he had only gone outside when the sun was up. Today is different. He has seized the day at its dawn and it is magnificent. The breath-taking greeting he has just received from the morning breeze is priceless. Like a king, Judah walks towards the garden. This is now his domain. The morning dew gives the soil richness in its colour. It looks beautiful. His eyes are definitely pleased with such a scenic sight. This garden had been there all these years, and each year, after his mother was gone, it had produced weeds. It was no longer going to be so.

Only yesterday, in one day, he had changed the look of the garden. Judah's mind races with charming thoughts of all the things he could do with this garden. He visualizes the garden full of spinach. Yes, green, leafy, shiny spinach. After that he would plant something else, maybe carrots or beans. It is at this moment that he resolves in his heart that never again will he allow the garden grow weeds as if it was incapable of producing good food.

Nothing can and will deter him now. For a while he stands in the middle of his garden mulling over ideas of what he can do with the garden. There is so much potential in it and it just needs someone to work it. It had never occurred to him before, but all of a sudden his eyes are open.

His mind is now made up that he would do whatever it takes to grow the spinach. If he fails to sell it at the big market, someone was definitely going to buy it because he was going to produce the best spinach.

"My spinach will sell because the labours of my hands are blessed". Today Judah does not doubt that whatever he does will prosper, because today, he is speaking from his heart. Judah smiles to himself at the thought that he is sounding like his mother, who spiritualized everything and thanked God for everything and anything.

Spinach Seeds

So, on the second day, Judah told himself he was going to plant his spinach seeds and that is exactly what he did.

The seed must die

The seeds were buried in the ground and while Judah could see nothing that was happening underneath the ground, Judah continued to water his garden every day. Judah was careful how he walked around the garden. After putting so much effort in it, he did not want to step on any seed.

The seed holds life.

The greatest discovery any man can make in life is to find the seed that he carries within himself. It is this very seed that unlocks success in life and allows a man to leave a legacy that perpetuates from one generation to the next. The seed on its own might look unattractive and might even be despised in terms of size, but never is a seed bigger than its fruit.

Two distinguished authors put it beautifully and wrote a book titled, "The forest in the seed[4]". *So if the seed holds so much potential within itself, why is it that not everyone goes about sowing the unique seeds they are carrying inside?*

Ever heard of the statement that: the graveyard is the richest place on earth[5]. It is a sad reality because so many people were born and they died without discovering their seed, later alone planting it. Without putting the seed to the ground, no matter what gimmicks a man may do, no matter what good intentions he may have, the seed will not and cannot produce after its own kind, until it is planted.

God in His ingenuity gave each man a unique seed. That seed is sufficient for his well being and more than enough to impact his sphere of influence and connect with the rest of humanity to complete the circle of life. Each and every person is born with purpose and carries that seed of purpose inside.

When man has no purpose, his life is void of expectation. Lack of purpose negates the reason to live or expectation of anything good happening in the future. It robs man of his will to live and to become. When a man finds a cause to die for, he finds his destiny.

A cause to die for does not always necessary mean that which is done at the expense of one's life but it simply means that which a man will pursue with all he has and strive to achieve no matter what it takes.

Chapter Seven

New beginnings...new life

It was not long after, that his dear father paid him a visit. His father always made it a point to visit him now and again. Even though he knew his son was not working, Judah's father never believed in spoon-feeding a grown up man. He never handed him anything on a silver platter. He frequently reminded him this by saying to him, "Son I gave you an education and I equipped you for life". So Judah had learnt over the years not to expect anything from his dad. He had sisters and brothers whom his father was still looking after, and Judah was wise enough not to ask his father for anything. And he rarely did.

Today particularly, Judah was feeling uneasy in his father's presence. His father was a good man, but he had his expectations from his son. Judah was not sure if his father would approve of his new venture. All his life he had never seen his father work in the garden. He did other odd jobs around the house, but he never worked in the garden. Judah remembered how his mother used to work in the garden and grow vegetables for the family. He wondered whether his mother ever bought vegetables when she was alive.

His mother had been such an industrious woman, always busy, always working and always encouraging him to read. He did not understand why God, the God his mother loved and believed in, had not healed her of the breast cancer. His question was never answered and eventually, he had come to accept that she was gone. For certainty, he would always, forever cherish the memory of her.

His mother always sang, always had a song on her lips. She said she wanted him to sing but Judah always had laughed and told her that he could not sing. He remembered how on his thirteenth birthday she gave him a guitar and told him to enjoy making music. It was the one gift he still had in its box. Despite the fact that his name means 'praise,'6 Judah never sang and he had never attempted to learn to play the guitar. What Judah liked to do was to scribble poems. He mused as he thought of his first poem to his father. His father had read the poem, looked at him and then said, "Son, I hope you don't want to make a career out of this". "No father," he had replied with a sheepish voice and with that, the first poem became the last poem, he wrote for his father.

"So now you've decided to become a farmer!" There was some sarcasm in the statement even though there was no malice on his father's face. On the contrary, there was pain on his face. His father looked very disappointed.

Judah ignored the pain on his father's face because did not like the tone of his father's voice. Instinctively he knew where his father was heading with this. If only his father would have faith in him and encourage him, it would mean the world to him. Judah resolved in his mind not to answer his father directly, so tactfully he said, "I can't sit and do nothing all day, at least this keeps me busy when I'm done with my job applications for the day". His father looked at him intently, then, lashed out words just as Judah was expecting.

With gout of anger stuck on his throat, Judah listened to his father, as he continued.

"Son, I have worked all my life and today I have no beefy inheritance to pass on to you when I die. You, your brothers and sisters will have to share what I have somehow and all my life savings will take care of your young sister's university fees. You cannot expect to start a family with a spinach garden. Look at yourself Son. I gave you an education that you can become somebody, not grow spinach. I worked hard all my life so that I could give my children a good education, so that you can be better than me in this life. What on earth has come over you, Son? Go out there and look for a job. Maybe you are not looking in the right places. Maybe you are not persistent enough. You need to knock on all doors until you get a job".

When he has said all he could say or rather all he wanted to say, Judah's father shakes his head, turns away and leaves Judah standing in the middle of his spinach garden.

Judah's heart is grieved by his father's outburst and his father's expressed disappointment. The words his father had spoken still ring in his head like the gong of the Catholic bell.

His head is spinning and a ball of anger burns in his throat. His eyes flash with tears. He is not a timid little boy anymore, so he holds those tears back. His loves his father but at this moment he does not dare say what he is feeling towards his father. It is better left unsaid because the last thing he wants to do is to curse the man he has respected for the greater part of his life.

Judah takes a deep breath and bends down resting both hands on his knees. As he straightens up he looks at the garden and kicks the dirt in front of him. He is not yet free from the echo of his father's voice. "This is worth trying!" he says as he bends over to feel the soil. It brings him little comfort. Even if it fails, at least he would have tried.

Judah understands what his father expects of him but he cannot live his life under his father's expectations anymore. He wonders if ever, in his lifetime, one day he would hear his father tell him that he was proud of him. He loves his father but he is not going abandon his garden just to please him. As he begins to walk back to the house, his eyes catch a glimpse of tiny shoots coming up the soil. Judah cannot believe his eyes. How had he missed it before? He walks row by row and crouching on the ground sees more tiny shoots of spinach that are celebrating life.

It's awesome.

The seeds are growing right before his eyes and these are his seeds, his spinach. Despite the fact that Judah has no one to share this joy with, at that moment, he allows himself to bellow out, "Yes, Yes!" as he beats the air with his fists.

Now his head is spinning with excitement. He can literally hear the orchestra of resounding joy all around him. The heavens seem to also celebrate the moment with him. He is on centre stage of great achievement. His heart is pounding with joy. It is an exhilarating moment. Judah leaps with joy careless of going overboard with such spontaneous merriment. This is too good to be true. This is a miracle for him.

During the days that follow, Judah faithfully works in his garden. He waters the garden and plucks out weeds. Each task energizes him and it is apparent that Judah is becoming a slave to his newly found passion. He gives it his full, undivided attention. He feels the soil in his hands very so often, as if to connect himself with the earth of his destiny. His mind is now set on achieving something he once never dreamt possible. With conscience discipline he does his daily tasks. It's as if suddenly he realizes that success is not for weak lazy people and success takes a lot of hard work and a lot of sacrifice.

He inspects each row day by day, taking his time to inspect every tender plant that is part of his garden, a part of his success. He becomes so engrossed with his garden that at times he speaks to the growing seeds. He engages them like they are living beings. Judah is sold out.

As the days unfold into seven-day weeks, Judah is now more rested within himself despite the hours he spends in the garden. He has inner peace and joy of accomplishment. The spinach is a delight to watch it grow. What Judah does not realize is that for the first time in his life he has done something that brings him inner fulfillment and he has done it not to please anyone but because he wanted to do it. What he is doing now resonates with his true self and that is what brings about the contentment.

Even though he does not articulate it now, it is his uncompromised commitment that is producing the results he is enjoying. His tenacious determination to make sure that no single plant dies makes him even more committed to work row by row. It is hard work, but, as far as Judah is concerned, it is worth it.

Chapter Eight

An opportunity presents itself

It is not long after that, that Judah's neighbour commends him for his garden and asks him if he is selling the spinach. Judah has not even pulled out any leaves to eat himself, so the question takes him by surprise. Nonetheless, Judah affirmatively responds. The next question also finds him unprepared because he has not yet placed a value tag on his spinach. Instead of giving a price himself, he jokingly throws the question to his neighbour, "How much would you pay to have a taste of this healthy-looking spinach?"

Judah's neighbour names his price, a price which Judah finds quite exorbitant for bundle of spinach, but wisely does not say anything except, "then we have a deal, when can I deliver the spinach?"

"Right-away!"

Judah starts plucking out the fresh leaves of spinach. His fingers shake slightly. With his back towards his neighbour, Judah avoids looking at his neighbour because he does not want him to see the grin on his face. After a while of plucking off the spinach leaves, the task seems easy enough but Judah continues doing it ever so gently as if he was handling a delicate baby. His neighbour immediately pays him upon receiving his bunch of spinach. With a smile on his face, as an after-thought he adds, "I'll let my friends know you are selling spinach". Before Judah can respond, his neighbour leaves the wall.

Judah is in business.

For a while Judah stands overwhelmed. He looks at the cash in his hand. There it was - the evidence that the labours of his hands are blessed. He had worked with his hands and now he is holding the fruit of his labours. Kneeling down, he kisses a spinach leaf and he kisses his hands. Before he knows what he is doing, Judah starts to sing. He has no clue where it is coming from, but the song just bubbles out of him. He does not care that maybe, someone might hear him sing.

The words just keep coming out of him. For a guy who had never sung much in his life, this is itself incredible. He is singing a song of thanksgiving. He gives thanks to God for his hands, the packet of seeds and for the garden. He thanks God for blessing the labours of his hands and for such beautiful spinach and the rich soil that works magic with seeds.

As he continues to sing, tears of joy roll down his cheeks. For the first time, in a long time, he has finally done something he can be proud of. The realization that he is capable of doing something with his life fills his heart with gratitude. He is grateful that he is not loser like he was feeling the past months. This moment means so much to him than he can express.

Right there in his garden Judah sings with joy. If his mother was alive this would have been one day she would have cried with him tears of joy.

It was yet another Judah-Spinach celebration and like the previous celebration, it just happened spontaneously. Here was evidence that a seed, that had been lying dormant within Judah, had finally found an outlet to express itself.

"I didn't know you could sing so beautifully", his neighbour says standing by the wall. Judah face flashes with embarrassment. He wonders how long his neighbour has been standing by the wall, as he replies, "I, I… didn't know I could sing myself, eh, it just happened".

For some reason his neighbour finds it so funny and he bellows a throaty laugh, which, too, makes Judah feel more embarrassed. "I'm sorry, but you remind me so much of myself when I was growing up. Anyway I came to get another bundle of spinach for myself; a friend of mine just took the one I bought few minutes ago".

While he plucks out more spinach leaves, Judah listens to his neighbour tell him how he had started writing books for children. It was amazing to hear the man talk. He had so much to say and he spoke with such eloquence that Judah wanted to hear more of what he was saying. As he hands him the spinach, the man is saying, "so you see I decided to do what I enjoyed doing and in the end I made some good money and I'm still making good money".

Judah humbly receives the money, thanks his neighbour twice and waits for his neighbour to take leave. But his neighbour does not leave right away. In fact, he seems to be in no hurry to leave. Does he expect Judah to offer him to jump over the wall and have a heart to heart chat with him? It's really an awkward moment for Judah. The prying neighbour keeps looking at Judah intently but does not say anything. As for Judah, he had seen that absorbed look before. That's how his father always looked at him when he wanted to say something serious to him. Judah feels uneasy because this is not his father and he does not even know this man's name.

Judah realizes that his neighbour is not going to leave him just yet, so he decides to look at his new acquaintance with father-son respect and holds his gaze for a while. The neighbour's look is not patronizing. On the contrary, his eyes hold so much peace and contentment that Judah thinks they have a sparkle in them.

"You know Son, not many people have the courage to follow their hearts these days. Young people like you will not be seen working in the garden or singing their hearts out in the back garden". There's a momentary pause before he continues. "It takes courage to be yourself and express the passion within you. When you are unafraid to be different from your peers, you unlock the potential that is hidden within you. It is that potential that makes great men, and it is the courage to be you, that separates the ordinary from the extraordinary. Just that extra courage makes the difference. Extraordinary men are ordinary men who are not afraid to express their passions, neither are they concerned about other people's opinions. Dreams are killed when people, especially the young people, do things out of other people's expectations and fail to follow their hearts.

Son, I can figure out that based on the excitement your eyes held when you sold your first bundle of spinach, you had never sold spinach before. This is also probably your first spinach garden, because I saw you kiss your spinach and your hands. I even saw your tears of joy. Son, what you have is passion and there are seeds within you that are waiting to be planted and produce real good fruit. Just as you planted your spinach seeds and they grew, plant your life and it will grow phenomenally."

Judah listens, tears welling up in his eyes. He listens to every word and hears every word. After speaking, his neighbour smiles at him, reaches out and taps on his shoulder twice and walks away.

It was like a well-planned sequel and Judah appreciates being left alone to absorb everything that he has just heard.

Who is this man?

Is it possible that Judah has come face to face with his set-man? He does not even know his name but something deep inside him connects him to this man. Listening to his neighbour had felt like hearing his father but there was more to it. His father had raised him up to be the young fine man he was today and this other father-figure seems to want to take him a step further. There's so much speculation in Judah's mind. Whatever has happened today is no coincidence. Everything that is unfolding is ushering him into his destiny, but Judah decides he will not spiritualize what has just happened.

Chapter Nine

Dejection and realization

When Judah answers his phone he knows immediately that his father is checking on him to find out about progress with the job hunt. Reluctantly Judah tells his dad that he has not yet found any administrative job. To put his father at ease, he assures him that he would let him know should anything come up. Before he hangs up, Judah gathers up his courage to tell his father that his spinach project is doing quite well. There is silence on the other side and Judah is lost as to what he should do next. He thinks he hears his father grunt, but he is not sure because the silence penetrates fear to his bones. "Dad are you still there", Judah dares to ask. "Son, I don't want to be the one to blow your bubble, but use all the hours you spent in that useless garden of yours looking for a decent job". Although he was expecting some rebuff, the words are very painful to hear. Ignoring his pain, Judah manages to say, "Goodbye Dad!"

His only wish for now is to have his father's approval. If only his father could see things from his perspective.

A month ago when people started coming to him for spinach, Judah thought people were just doing it to support him, as a friendly neighbourhood gesture. After a while, he came to know that his spinach was really good and people were buying because they were getting value for their money. His crinkly leafy spinach was so good that it was actually making people want more of it. He was not sure if he could keep up with demand, because some rows were getting bare as each day passed. It was all good but the thought that his father did not share in his success nagged upon his heart to the point of sorrow.

His father was judging him by his past and it was not fair on him. His own father saw him as an incompetent boy who did not have the guts to finish what he starts. His father was wrong because he was a different Judah. He was a Judah, who was passionate and determined to achieve something with his life. How was his father ever going to know the really Judah if he was not willing to give him a chance. Judah determined that day that he was not going to allow his past to define him. He was not who his father thought he was and with or without his father's support, he was going to pursue his passion. Yes his father had raised him and he had done the best he could, but that was not going to trap him into aborting his newly found passion. His father would just have to be out of the picture of his progression, if it was going to come to that. Nothing was going to change the fact that he is his father's son. The only reality that mattered to him right now was pursuing his dream and growing the seed that was germinating in his innermost being.

Feeling a bit watered down emotionally, Judah begins to wonder why his neighbour has not come to the wall for almost a week. He had however caught glimpse of the neighbour's wife picking flowers but not him.

Judah toys with the idea of visiting his neighbour but he is not really sure if he should visit him without an appointment. He misses his father but he cannot call him especially after the last call. Maybe it was pride, but on the other hand, he wanted to avoid another outburst from his dad. Maybe they both needed their space away from each other. Judah desperately needs someone to talk to just to and it is on this premise of thought that he decides to visit his neighbour.

As soon as he presses the green intercom button, the gate starts to slide open for him. He can't help but notice that the yard is immaculately clean. The lawn is well manicured. The trees, the shrubs and every other growing plant are neatly trimmed and pruned. Judah's eyes are astonished by the beauty of the flowers that are planted parallel the driveway. Not a single leaf is on the ground. Everything looks perfect to him. He feels like he is standing in the middle of an enchanted garden. There's so much for his eyes to take in and the beauty of it all is just too much to absorb all at once.

Judah decides not to go straight to the front door instead he chooses to use the back door. Here too, everything is neat as a pin. Then lo and behold, Judah sees his neighbour's vegetable garden. It is the most exquisite vegetable garden he has ever seen. It is an all season garden that, from his garden, looks like a big well-built shed. It has seven beds and each bed has a different vegetable. There is a bed of lettuce and another one of carrots, another with onion, and another has beans. The next has tomato, the next seem to be potatoes and the seventh bed has spinach, just like his spinach. Judah stands awe-struck and meanwhile a thousand thoughts race through his mind.

Jolting back to reality he suddenly remembers that he has come to visit and that perhaps the person who opened the gate for him is probably watching him. A tinge of awkwardness colour his face as he makes his way to the back door. A friendly lady, he recognizes to be the woman he sees from his garden, opens the door for him before he knocks. He politely greets her with a sheepish smile and he cannot help but notice that her eyes are glowing as if she is about to burst out laughing, but she does not laugh.

Patting his hand warmly she gently lets him know, "he's been expecting you for three days now". Judah is surprised to hear that but he does not have ample time to look surprised. The gentle motherly touch of this woman, reminds him of his mother. It's a soothing touch and until now he has not realized just how much he misses a mother's love. He indulges himself a moment to cherish this gesture and hands her the small package he has brought with him. He is glad that he had brought the gift, just as his mother had taught him long ago. Never go to someone you respect empty-handed. Always take a gift, no matter how small it may be. He was glad he remembered. His mother was right.

"Who are these people?" he wonders.

As he is ushered into the living room, Judah is intrigued by the fact that everything is in its place and looks just right. He wonders if anything is used or if they are children in the house. If indeed they were children, how did they always keep everything in its place like this? His first question was not immediately answered but his second question is answered when a sweet voice calls from the other room asking who has come to see them. The neighbour's wife smiles at him and lets out a warm laugh and he knows that the child will be attended to shortly.

His neighbour watches him come towards him. In his home, this man is king and there is a sense of royalty all around him. His humble demeanor is not easily visible but neither is he arrogant. As he extends his hand to Judah, his eyes remain fixed on his visitor. Judah is given one hundred percent attention as if he is some important dignitary. Conscious of the atmosphere this man creates Judah straightens up his shoulders and likewise stretches out his hand to give his neighbour a handshake.

"I was beginning to wonder about you'" he says as they exchange the handshake. It's a firm business-like handshake. Judah does not really know how to respond to him but decides to say, "It's good to see you Sir." Even though he was not sure of how to begin talking to this man, he is sure within himself that he can talk to this man almost about anything and everything.

Judah quietly accepts the seat that is offered to him and mumbles a thank you as he relaxes into the settee. His neighbour seats himself in a position that makes it clear that he wants to have a heart to heart chat with him.

Judah clears his throat but before he says what was on his mind, his neighbour takes the lead and speaks first.

"Son, I guess the most awkward thing for you right now is that you don't know how to address me. I've seen you with your father now and again, so I know you have a father. Most youngsters call me 'Pa'. My friends call me Christo and my wife calls me Christopher only when I have forgotten to do something for her. But you can decide what you want to call me, but I'll call you 'Son' if you don't mind."

Judah's mind juggles several words, sir, dad, pa, uncle, teacher, but none of them seem to quite flow with him.

"Is it Ok if I call you Abba-Chris?" Judah blurts out.

Neither is the hearer nor the speaker amply prepared for such question.

"Is Judah aware that the word 'Abba' is the most intimate way you can address a father in the Jewish culture, an equivalent to 'Daddy'?" Abba-Chris wonders.

There is a prolonged moment of silence before Judah receives his answer.

"You know Son, if that is what is coming from your heart, then Abba-Chris it is".

Is he seeing right or is he mistaken that they are tears in Abba-Chris's eyes? If they are tears, Abba-Chris does not make any effort to wipe them but allows them to naturally clear away. It is an unusual emotional moment for some reason, as if the prodigal son has just come home and his father is overwhelmed by love.

The afternoon went by so fast. Abba-Chris's wife, whom Judah decided he would address as 'Ma' brought them refreshments. Two children came and asked his name at one point during his visit and he gladly told them and they scampered out of the room giggling. Judah listened when Abba-Chris talked. Abba –Chris asked him probing questions and listened so attentively when he spoke. He listened acknowledging with a nod, a word or a gesture appropriately as he saw fit. It was obvious to Judah that this man knew, understood and applied effective communication skills. He had so much he wanted to ask but Abba-Chris assured him that there was plenty of time ahead of them.

As he beads farewell to his hosts, Ma gives him a tight hug and hands him some cookies and Abba- Chris gives him a pat on the shoulder.

There is just one more question Judah cannot resist asking before he leaves.

"Abba-Chris, why do you buy my spinach when you have spinach and your spinach is just like mine?

"Son, you need to know when to make a good investment and my money coming to your pocket is a good investment on my part. You benefit on one side, while on my side my returns are always greater that my initial investment". He smiles and offers no further explanation but the expression on his face tells Judah that with time he is going to figure it out.

Everything is about a seed. Every day and every time man is sowing seeds.

Abba-Chris decided to sow into Judah's work because as far as he knew, it was good soil. It was his initial sowing into this young man's life that had connected them. He did not need the spinach but he wanted a relationship and already that seed had now given him more than a bundle of spinach, it had given him a son.

A man reaps what he sows. He who does not sow shall not reap in the time of harvest. He who sows sparingly shall reap sparingly and he who sows unsparingly will likewise reap unsparingly.7 The quality of the seed that is sown determines the quality of the harvest that is gathered.

Chapter Eleven

Time to learn

There was an understanding between the two of them that strengthened their relationship. While they had different personalities, they complimented one another, were like-minded and enjoyed being together. Judah watched as Abba-Chris helped his wife prepare the salad. Unlike his father, Abba-Chris found nothing wrong with doing the so-categorized women chores. Later on Judah learnt that Abba-Chris did such chores just to be next to his wife and having the pleasure of doing with her what she enjoyed doing.

Judah's parents had been married for thirty-two years before his mother passed away and he knew his mother had been happy. She always used to speak highly of her husband and used to say, "Judah I hope you learn from your father how to treat the woman you will marry. Your father has his faults, like all of us, but he is a good husband to me."

Judah had laughed and told his mother that he was not yet thinking of marriage, but he promised to watch his father. Judah had since then, until his mother's death, watched how his father treated his mother. From then he had started to notice how his father respected his mother and never failed to say thank you for everything she did for him, no matter how small. He saw them hold hands, take walks together, read books together, laugh and eat together. He never corrected or rebuked her in their presence and yet he took every opportunity to compliment her in their presence. He did not see his father argue with his mother but he knew they had their moments of ironing things out in the privacy of their bedroom. One such moment when they had disagreed was when he enrolled into college. He had overheard them talk about it and his mother still felt he had imposed his decision on Judah, but his father argued otherwise. On that issue they had agreed to disagree. His mother had submitted to his father, just as he obeyed his father's final word.

Now he watched Abba-Chris and wondered where these men of his father's generation had acquired so much wisdom. They seemed to be men governed by sets of principles on which they developed their individual philosophy of life. They were not wishy-washy, but instead, took a bold stance on ideology and religiously followed it through. His father always told him to walk with his ears and eyes open. He remembered his father telling him to be always aware of his environment and to give an ear when people spoke, especially the elderly. He was privileged to know such men especially during this time. He wanted their wisdom, but, he wanted it in a greater measure. He told himself that if ever he found the source for such wisdom he would trade everything he had to get it. His father told him that wisdom was everywhere, but not everyone could identify it. Maybe Abba-Chris could tell him how to identify and get a hold of it. Judah knew the secret of getting answers. It was to ask.

When Abba-Chris joins him, Judah simply asks, "how do you do it Abba-Chris, how do you manage to juggle so many things and still get everything right?"

"It does not come easy, Son. It has taken me a lifetime to be where I am today. One secret though is build precept upon precept. When you learn something, learn it well, apply it and use it to your advantage."

"Don't learn things for the sake of head knowledge because it only gives you a big head. Learn to advance yourself so that you are equipped to improve the lives of people around you because that will, in turn, create your significance. It's noble to become a success, but there is greater glory in becoming significant".

He laughs as he recalls something. "You know I have not always been so clever. There were things I learnt the hard way. I remember one day my father giving me money to go and pay one of his bills. I took the money and I ran to pay but I was told it's a dollar short and I could not pay the bill. I went back to my father who handed me a dollar before I could say anything. He told me to go back and pay the bill. When I came back he said to me, 'Son, I gave you money and you did not count it, but you counted it when you were told it's a dollar short. You wasted time coming back to me and time going back again, precious time we could have used for something else. Money like time holds value, so whenever you receive money or work with figures, check it and if you are a wise guy, triple check it, you will save yourself lots of time.' From that time I learnt that one useful skill in life is simply to pay attention to detail".

Chapter Twelve

Two hands are better than one

Judah appreciated having another set of hands to help him with the work. During the past weeks work had just seemed to be piling up in front of him. There was so much to be done and it seemed like there was so little time to get it all done. Despite the amount of work that had to be done, Judah did not regret the decision that he had made. It definitely had not been easy for him, but he did what was best for him and probably for his family in the near future.

He did not see much of his brothers and sisters these days, but he made it a point to call them once in a while just to check on them. They too, had so much going on for them, in their individual worlds. A part of him missed his father and he planned to visit him this coming weekend. The past three weekends he had been so busy with work, that he had not even had time to himself. So much had not happened in the year, when he had no work, and yet so much had happened in the same year, within a short space of time. Judah's conclusion to this was that the opening of one opportunity, if handled correctly, has a way of unlocking doors to other bigger opportunities.

Jeff was working steadily. He had a firm hand and his muscular body seemed comfortable and at ease as he dug the remaining part of the fallow ground. Already he had dug out much of the lawn as per Judah's instructions. While he was doing the digging, Judah was busy preparing the rows for the new spinach.

Judah was grateful that he had listened to one of his customers who had advised him to create more space for the garden. The woman had chuckled, after suggesting that Judah should dig out the lawn if he needed more space. She had further said that if he still needed more space, then he could use her garden for a small fee in return.

The same woman had also said, "Don't wait till the last minute to realize that you have no more spinach to sell. It would be a shame."

Judah had listened and after-all it made good sense to do something before it was too late, especially now, considering that he had forgone taking the assistant accountant position.

He had no regrets, except he only hoped that one day his father would come to acknowledge the wisdom behind his decision.

Spinach growing was laborious, but it brought him satisfaction. His hands enjoyed it. He could not yet call himself a farmer but he liked what he was doing and he was now planning to find more land to plant more spinach. Judah also planned to be able to plant spinach all year round. As a result of his big plans, he started researching as much as he could on spinach growing.

Judah also began to talk to people about how he could get more land to use without, at this moment in time, buying the land for himself. He did not have the capital to invest in land. All the money he was making so far, he was putting back into his venture.

Judah's eyes were all of a sudden open to see idle gardens. Whenever he walked around his neighbourhood, he wanted to see what people were doing with their gardens. So many people had gardens but most of them were not using their gardens. If only gardens were something he could borrow and carry to his home, he would do just that. Judah wanted more land to grow more spinach than he ever dreamt possible.

Chapter Thirteen

Looking forward

Abba-Chris was a great inspiration. He allowed Judah to ask questions and he answered Judah's questions. Many times his answers came camouflaged in his life's experiences. He taught him what he had learnt over the years.

What he shared were principles that he himself was using in his life. Abba-Chris freely told Judah as much as he knew, as long as it was relevant to what they were talking about. He was prepared to lift Judah on his shoulders, so that Judah could see horizons he himself had never seen. Judah did not have to re-invent the wheel of success. All he had to do was apply the principles others had discovered and used and achieved their success.

He told Judah not to be ashamed of asking questions and not be afraid of trying. Judah took comfort in knowing that even if he failed in his venture, at least he would live knowing that he had at one point in his life, followed his heart. If he did fail, Judah was not going to regret having tried because it was not out of frustration that he made the decision to follow his heart. That being said, Judah was not prepared to fail. He did not want to fail.

Chapter Fourteen

More than a dream

The applause was ear deafening. He had never seen so many famous people in one place. These were great successful people in different fields, but he had no clue who they were. And there he was standing before them. After the applause, silence prevailed in the great hall. "Ladies and gentlemen" the man next to him said, "Thank you for coming tonight, Thank you for your support. As you leave tonight, you will each receive a recipe book with over 150 creative spinach recipes. Enjoy your spinach ladies and gentlemen and good night!' The people applauded again, but this time, louder than before. It was so thunderous that it woke Judah up.

He was in his bed.

It was just a dream but to Judah it was more than a dream. It was a vision that penetrated deeper beyond his soul. In fact it was so big that he needed to tap into every reserve of his potential. With this dream Judah decided that he would make demands upon himself that he had never made before. He was going to achieve the impossible. This was another seed he was going to plant, if not tomorrow, definitely somewhere in the near future. Something new would be birthed that was going to change the story of the green leaves commonly known as spinach.

Judah's mind had been triggered to succeed and deep within himself he knew that nothing was going to stop him. He could only stop himself and he was not going to. There was so much he could do with spinach. It was that same night that Judah decided that he was not going to grow anything else except spinach. He was going to focus all his attention, resources and energy on growing spinach and see just how far he could go with it.

The blessing comes in its fullness when you align yourself with your purpose. You begin to produce a 100-fold when you are producing that which was placed inside you from the time of your conception. If it is coming from inside you, you can never fail. You may face challenges but as long as you keep producing from within, the floodgates will open and you will see the blessing overtake you. You may call it a gift or a talent but it's the thing that God placed inside as your resource to draw from, to attain significance and live a purpose-driven life.

Chapter Fifteen

Crystallizing the passion

This time when Judah's father comes to see his son, he finds a van parked in front of the house with Jeff and Judah loading spinach onto it. Judah immediately stops what he was doing and goes to meet his father. If his father is surprised, he does not express it, as he greets his son. He looks around only to find out there is spinach growing literally everywhere.

As he walks around, to his uttermost astonishment, Judah has used every bit of ground to plant spinach. That just does it. This sparks his father and he begins to laugh so loud. Judah doesn't know what to make of it. His father goes around the house again, this time on his own.

When he rejoins Judah, he is still bewildered. "I wish your mother was here to see this. You are really sold out on this spinach, aren't you Son?"

"Yes Dad, I guess I am", Judah replies looking his father respectfully in the eyes. He is not ashamed to be who he is, or with what he has become and what he is becoming in the process of following his heart. Judah is now so determined to keep on producing that which is inside him that he is no longer afraid to express himself through his work. Even though Judah is working with his hands to plant spinach, he is ultimately defining his destiny. His hands are merely instruments being coordinated by what is inside him. As a result of being true to himself he is yielding results that are evident to all.

"I enjoy planting spinach;

I enjoy watching it grow before my very eyes.

I enjoy seeing people enjoy buying it.

I like the smell of it and the feel of it.

It's absolutely tender.

I connect with the soil;

And I like to see my hands dirty.

Spinach inspires me to sing while I work,

So I sing while I am working,

And before I know it, my day's work is done.

I want to plant more spinach,

And grow as much as I can,

And discover the real me in the process.

I want every household to eat my spinach.

Dad, I know this is not what you wanted for me. I know you wanted something better for me but this is the best for me. Spinach is best for me. I will not deny myself this because this is who I am and whether the world applauds it or not, I will do it because it makes me happy."

Never before in his life had Judah's father heard his son speak so boldly and with such fervor. He could sense the passion that came forth with each word, as it left his son's lips. Judah's speech exudes confidence that he knows what he is doing and is will do much more than this. It is obvious to his dad now that he is never going to look back.

Strangely enough he is proud of Judah, but at this point in time, he does not have the guts to tell his son.

"I won't take much of your spinach time Son, but I'll definitely bring your brothers and sisters over tomorrow for them to see this wonder." If there was sarcasm in his father's voice, Judah did not pick it. It was hard to read his father's emotions, so he decided not to come any conclusions.

"That will be great Dad, bye now". As he walks his father to the car, his father turns around to look at the spinach one more time and shakes his head. There's a slight smile on his face but he does not say anything. Judah hopes his father would leave him with an encouraging word but for now his wish is not granted. He was a good father but it baffles Judah why it was so difficult for him to be part of his dream or to just be happy for him.

Judah decides that tomorrow, since his two brothers and two sisters are coming over, it would be nice to prepare a family lunch and definitely have some Judah-spinach ready for them to taste.

Chapter Sixteen

The Test

Judah was definitely beginning to feel frustrated. He was out of his depth and he had not envisioned that the land application would be so difficult and time consuming. He was not sure he could pursue it further. Being ambitious was good but maybe he had just bitten a big chunk he could not chew. The frustration was building up in him feelings that he knew would leave him bitter and discouraged, if he did not do something about it quickly.

It was as if barriers and blockades were deliberately being put before him to stop him from getting land. So many questions, so many obstacles and so many other technicalities he was not prepared for, kept popping up.

He was just a young man who wanted some land to grow more spinach. The system in place and people employed to man these offices were terribly rigid. To avoid cursing procedures and systems, Judah decides that it's prudent to talk to Abba-Chris before going further. As it is, he no longer has the willpower to go further. Discouragement had set in and doom was looming over him ready to destroy his dream once and for all.

Judah cannot stop the tears and does not seem to mind crying in front of Abba-Chris. Until now, Judah had not realized just how frustrated he is. He knew he was frustrated but he had no idea that the frustration had taken root in him and was developing into a gangrene of unexpressed anger. Now that he has someone who cares to listen to him, all the pain floods his heart and he cries his heart out.

Abba-Chris allowed him to cry.

Judah wept.

Men don't cry. No, actually strong men cry. It takes guts for a man to cry and that was the reason why Abba-Chris allowed Judah to cry it out and get it out.

Abba-Chris now listens as Judah narrates his frustrations. He listens until Judah has said all he wanted to say. Judah is upset with the systems of government administration. The apathy he had received from some people and the ridicule in some offices. He expresses how he felt rejected as if his spinach venture was mere play. He felt belittled and disadvantaged that he did not have money to just buy a farm without having to make applications for land.

His frustration is further compounded by negative thoughts in his head telling him that at this point in his life he is making a fool himself. The voices of discouragement were loud and based their accusations on reality. The facts grimace at him and logically speaking there is no way he is going to get the results he wanted.

What was he thinking all along when he thought he could build an empire from a spinach garden? Was it really a gift to be able to grow spinach?

Anyone could plant spinach if they wanted to.

He is good with figures – maybe that is his gift. Maybe that was what his father had tried to tell him all along and he had not listened. Instead he had chosen not to listen because bookkeeping did not excite him. He could have been an accountant, but he had just been too big-headed to heed his father's voice. This was torture to his mind and soul. How did he think he could step out in faith, when all his life he had despised his mother's faith? It was incredulously silly of him to think that he could grasp the fundamentals of living by faith overnight. He was his father's son and his father was a man of logic. What had come over him to grow spinach instead of balancing books and drawing up financial statements?

Had he missed his gift in the quest for wanting to be fulfilled? Judah was so messed up within himself that he was not sure what he wanted anymore. He kicked himself for following his heart. He asked himself over and over again, "what was I thinking planting spinach and thinking I had found my pearl?" He undeniably felt like an idiot at this moment in time. He must have begun to sound like one because abruptly Abba-Chris stops him from self-condemnation and self-destructive talk.

He had never heard Abba-Chris speak like that before. Abba-Chris' rebuke was blunt. "Get a hold of yourself Son, you must never allow your feelings to rule your heart. Never give your emotions that privilege because if you do, it will destroy all you have achieved to date".

Judah knows that Abba-Chris's eyes are fixed on him and he cannot continue behaving like a wimp. With much courage on his part, he raises his head until his eyes meet Abba-Chris's. There is no condemnation in those eyes, just love and understanding. He knows that Abba-Chris can write him a million dollar cheque right now for a farm, and all his problems will be sorted out, but he also knows that Abba-Chris would not do that for his sake. Abba-Chris wants Judah to be a man of character and a man of substance. It was times such as this one that is the furnace of moulding such character.

Abba-Chris voice is now gentler than before.

"Listen Son", he says, "*which man intending to build a tower, does not sit down first and count the cost, whether he has enough to finish it, just in case after he has laid the foundation, and is not able to finish, all who see it begin to mock him, saying, 'this man began to build and was not able to finish'.*"

Abba-Chris straightens up, takes Judah's hands to his hands and says, "Son, your gift is not in spinach, your gift is in these hands".

Judah looks at his hands as if he is seeing them for the very first time. "The labours of your hands will be blessed". His mother had always told him that. Still looking at his hands, Judah thinks of his mother and wonders why his mother had never preached to him about her God. 'Maybe she had', he thinks, 'maybe she preached to me every day and I just missed her whole life sermon'.

Abba-Chris lets go his hands and Judah clasps his hands together and brings them to his chest. He feels at ease as if a heavy burden has been lifted off his chest. Abba-Chris must have signaled his wife because she soon enters with a tray of refreshments for them.

Chapter Seventeen

Placed in the correct hands

Jeff worked hard. He was always there early morning and worked throughout the day. He took his lunch breaks and ate whatever Judah had for lunch.

Judah had had the time to sit done and count the cost of pursuing his heart's dream. Now he had his vision written out and if anything happened, if the storms came or he faced obstacles, he promised himself that he would read his vision. From now on his vision was to influence his decisions. Through the course of the past weeks his vision had become engraved on his heart. He had a clear picture of what he wanted and even though the vision seemed too big for him, Judah was confident that he would find help on the way. His vision was so big it would take him a lifetime to accomplish. He was no longer thinking small, now Judah was thinking of generations. He wanted to impact generations.

Judah now watches Jeff working. Jeff always worked quietly. He did not say much but he smiled a lot. Judah wonders about Jeff's unique seed. Instead of just wondering Judah thinks it's best to find out.

"Jeff, if we were living in a perfect world where you could do anything you wanted, what would you do?"

Jeff smiles and replies politely "but it's not a perfect world Judah."

He is right based on his circumstances and his level of understanding, but Judah does not accept that answer because he knows better. Judah now knows that one creates their own reality by what they do or fail to do. He now understands that through thoughts man frames his world. He also knows, from what Abba-Chris had told him on the day of his breakdown, that words have power to create what is spoken. Life-giving words produce life and negative words undoubtedly reap an equivalent harvest of death.

Judah now knows that each person, including Jeff, has a gift and unless that gift is used, it will lie dormant. If never used, sadly enough, the same untapped gift will die inside the person, never having been activated.

Judah thinks about the number of people who sacrifice their dreams because of fear. They live in the shadows of other men because it's safe. Even though it's a sad reality, thousands and thousands will continue to do so and remain okay with it. Judah knows that he cannot change the world but he is aware that if he can change one man's life, someone like Jeff, he would have changed a family and maybe, if Jeff does well, the generation of the lineage of Jeff would be changed.

"Ok Jeff it's not a perfect world, but I know there is one thing you would want to do if you were given a chance. What is that one thing?"

Jeff looks at Judah but as his eyes met with Judah's, he quickly looks away then looks on the ground and sheepishly replies, "play the guitar!"

Judah cannot envision Jeff playing a guitar but one can *never judge a book by its cover* and definitely no one, by looking at a person, can tell what that person's gift is.

Without a word, Judah immediately goes into the house and a few minutes later comes out with a long rectangular box that had only been opened once. Jeff has gone back to his work and does not see Judah come out. He is startled when Judah calls his name. With an attitude of instant obedience, Jeff drops his spade and walks towards Judah. Judah seems very happy with himself. His face is beaming but he does not give away a smile.

"I want you to have this". Jeff is about to receive the package but noticing that his hands are very dirty he stops. Using eye communication, Judah gives Jeff time for him to go and wash his hands.

It is the most beautiful guitar Jeff has ever seen. Jeff had never received an expensive gift from anyone before and he is lost for words.

"It's so, it's so…."

"It's yours now. I want you to have it but first play something for me."

Judah notices that Jeff's hands are shaking as he takes the guitar. He removes it so gently from the box as if he was handling a newly-born baby.

After finding a spot to sit down, Jeff positions the guitar on his lap and all the while Judah is amazed by the grace with which his fingers prepare themselves to play. Jeff's fingers dance with excitement as they feel the strings. It is in the fingers. Jeff's gift was hidden in those fingers. Taking a momentary pause, Judah realizes just how creative and ingenious the Creator of man is. He hides people's gifts in the most obvious places yet many people never find the gift or do they and complacency robs them of it? Different hands are gifted differently. Judah looks at Jeff's fingers with bewilderment as a melody begins.

He plays softly. Judah does not know what tune is being played, but as he watches Jeff's fingers move he can sense the thrill vibrating from them. It is sensational. Never in a million years, could he have guessed Jeff's fingers could do what they are doing now. Jeff plays with his eyes closed and with a smile on his face. He looks so happy, so alive. In fact, Judah realizes that he has never seen Jeff so at peace with himself, as he is now. It makes him want to cry. He has to share this with someone. He has to make some people hear Jeff play. It would be selfishness to enjoy it by himself. Judah concludes that it is also sin for Jeff to deny the world this gift.

Judah is thinking the healing this kind of music can bring to minds in turmoil. The nerves this music can calm. The joy this music can unleash. He is thinking that if only…. the music stops. No, the music must go on. Jeff puts the guitar in the box and closes the lid. He hands the box back to Judah and Judah notices that there are tears in Jeff's eyes. Something was hurting Jeff so deep and Judah has no clue of knowing what it is. Judah is also clueless about what to say.

Jeff walks away and picks up his spade as if this beautiful moment never took place. He goes to work and do something that puts food on his table. Judah is oblivious as to why Jeff is acting this way. Judah does not know that in the past Jeff had played but his playing had just entertained people and enriched the rich but had brought him neither riches nor fame. A part of Judah is stunned and a part of him feels deep sorrow. He is no Abba-Chris and therefore he is not ready to deal with this. Judah thinks, 'if only Abba-Chris had been here to listen to Jeff play and see what had just taken place, he would definitely know how to handle it.

Jeff is now busy with his work, but Judah knows Jeff's heartache would remain for a while. Judah understands what it feels like to have your heart ache. He wants to reach out to this guy and help him but he just has no clue how to do that.

Judah looks at Jeff and then at the box in his hands. As long as that guitar remained in that box, no tune was going to come from it. Jeff could bring music out of it, but now, who was going to bring Jeff out of his past and usher him into the future?

Chapter Eighteen

Tough Reality

Abba-Chris listens, as always, attentively as Judah speaks to him about Jeff. Judah speaks with feeling because he is very fond of Jeff. He remembered the day Jeff had come to him. Jeff had offered to work for the day and in return get a plate of hot food. Judah had at that time not planned to hire anyone to help him with his garden. It was because of the earnestness in Jeff's eyes that he had given him work to do. As Jeff had begun working, Judah had started preparing a hot meal for him. He cooked more than enough for one meal. He cooked extra so that Jeff could have take-away for supper. He had watched Jeff devour his food and afterwards he received a heartfelt thank you. The quality of gratitude Jeff extended to him that first day was more than he could ask for. It held a message that he valued the giver more than he valued the plate of food. It was because of the quality of appreciation he received from Jeff that day, that made Judah offer Jeff a job.

By the time Judah finishes talking to Abba-Chris, Abba-Chris has no doubt as to how Judah feels about Jeff.

"So what do you want me to do?" Abba-Chris asks Judah.

"I want you to do for Jeff what you did for me".

Judah's request is clear and straight-forward.

It was because of Abba-Chris that Judah he had come to appreciate who he was. This man sitting with him was his guide, a mentor and a father who taught him life principles. He wanted the same for Jeff, so that Jeff could become all he could be.

"I can't do that," Abba-Chris responds without taking his eyes off Judah. Judah, although he was looking at Abba-Chris, now intently looks at Abba-Chris, with a frown of confusion on his brow. Abba-Chris does not twitch but he repeats himself to make himself very clear to Judah, "Son, I can't do what you are asking me to do. I did it for you but I cannot do it for Jeff."

There is such finality in that voice that if Judah did not have a relationship with Abba-Chris he would have walked away. Not only was there finality in the voice but there was sharpness to his tone of voice.

Abba-Chris waits.

Judah waits.

Judah waits to compose his emotions, so that whatever he says next comes out correctly, without wrong emotion. Abba-Chris waits so that Judah hears what he is saying and accepts his reply as final.

So they both wait.

There is no tension between the two, but Judah wants to understand. Abba-Chris cannot just say, "No". He wants an explanation and he wants to understand why he is saying "no" when he has seen him teach so many other people. What is wrong with him teaching Jeff? Abba-Chris is always there for people who come to him, never turning anyone away, so he wants to understand why then can Abba-Chris not help Jeff.

"Why are you saying, "No", Abba-Chris?" Judah asks after engaging his guts.

"Why are you questioning my decision?"

"Because it does not make sense to me and I want to understand. I want to understand why you don't want to help Jeff?" Judah speaks as a son who has every right to learn from his father.

"It's very simple Son. You are asking me to help someone who did not come to me for my help. Remember how I waited for you to come to me after I had introduced myself to you. I cannot impose myself on anyone and I will not do it. I wait for the invitation. How do you know Jeff wants this help as badly as you want it for him? Did I not tell you the other day that you must never throw your pearls to the swine? I know you are feeling sorry for Jeff, but if he does not want to change and become who he is meant to be, it does not matter who talks to him and what you give him, he will never change. Change starts when a man makes a personal decision to change. It must be a desire from within, not one that is imposed on him by anyone".

Judah is enlightened but he is also offended that Abba-Chris compared Jeff to a swine.

"But Jeff is not a swine. He is a good guy who probably has never been given a chance in life… but he is a good guy". Judah speaks more to convince himself and not so much convince Abba-Chris.

Since the day he had played the guitar, Jeff now kept a safe distance from Judah. He had not accepted the guitar, so Judah had put the guitar back in its place. Jeff still did his work steadily but something had definitely changed and it bothered Judah.

Chapter Nineteen

Open doors

It was an unexpected call but his father wanted to meet with him that afternoon without fail. Judah promised to meet his father and without saying anything further, his father hung up. If there was anything his father wanted from him or wanted to speak to him on a serious note, his father always arranged to come to Judah. Judah wondered why this time it was different.

He expected to find his father alone but to his surprise his father was in the company of his young brother and two other gentlemen. The one gentleman was a familiar face. It was one of father's friends but he did not know the other gentleman. After the formalities of greeting had been done, his father wasted no time but got to the point of why he had called him for the meeting.

His father spoke of how he had watched him work consistently and relentlessly on his spinach venture. How despite the challenges he met along the way, he had overcome each challenge. He confessed how he had asked his younger brother to keep him abreast with what was going on with him. At that Judah looked at his younger brother and smiled an "I'll catch you later for that" smile. His father went on to talk about how when he saw the spinach growing all around the house, he realized just how serious and important this venture was to him.

Judah listened to his father's narration of events of the spinach venture. Until now he had no clue that his father took interest in what he was doing. His father also spoke of his relationship with Mr. Zebulun and how grateful he was that Judah had such a mentor in his life. Judah had mentioned Abba-Chris to his father, but he was not aware that his father knew just how close he was to Abba-Chris. He commended his son for having a teachable heart to learn from such a great man. At that juncture, his friend elaborated on some of Abba-Chris's accomplishments, which Judah was only hearing for the first time.

For some time Abba-Chris became the subject of the meeting. It was now obvious to Judah that not only was Abba-Chris a hero in his life, but Abba-Chris's influence on people and the community was immeasurable. Abba-Chris was a living legend, yet he was so down to earth. His father had admiration for that man and his father was man-enough to give honour where honour was due.

His father then continued as to how one day he had spoken to his friend, now sitting on his left side, about the blooming spinach venture and in turn his friend had asked his father, "So why don't you help your son find land?"

His father had thought about it and they had both agreed that they would do what they could to assist Judah get more land. Sometime later, his father's friend had visited an old friend out of town and lo and behold he had seen land lying idle. The land belonged to this other gentleman, sitting with them now, who had been contemplating on selling but had not yet made up his mind at that time. Upon hearing this, his father had been in touch with his friend's friend and convinced him to sell the land. Judah listened to his father with admiration. He could sense excitement building up within him. "Your father is a good man", he remembered his mother saying over and over again. Judah now understood why his mother said it over and over again. His father was a good man. He had a good heart.

If Judah was interested, his father continued to explain, it would mean they trade in one house as a down payment and then agree on terms to pay off the balance within a short period of time. Mr. Wilson, to whom the farm belonged, now spoke and said, "I'd be happier if I could have all the money in within two years". Judah quickly did the calculations in his head. Paying the balance over two years would definitely be steep, but despite that, the deal still sounded good. No one said anything further, but Mr. Wilson intuitively knew that his point would be taken into consideration.

His father concluded by telling Judah that the Wilsons were willing to vacate the farm as soon as he was ready to vacate the house and pay the first installment.

Judah looked at his father for a long while and now that the cards were laid on the table, his father's friend and Mr. Wilson excused themselves to allow Judah and his father the privacy they needed to make a final decision.

Left with his father and brother Judah is short for words. He is surprised and overwhelmed by what his father has done for him.

"Thank you Father", Judah says breaking the silence, "I don't really know what to say".

"I realized that it was more than growing spinach for you, Son".

Judah assures his father that the deal is good and that he has no problem giving up the house at any time. His only concern is that he does not know just how soon he can raise the first installment. Even though the spinach venture was doing well, it was not yet at the level of giving him the amount that was required for the deposit. As Judah does his mental projections and calculations his father also weighs his options.

His father interrupts his thoughts by telling him that as a family they are willing to help him with the deposit. His father is also prepared to invest his life's savings into the farm but his only fear is that if it does not work out, then his sisters' education fund would be jeopardized. His father could also possibly apply for a loan at his company. Judah again is surprised by his father's willingness to do all that only so that he gets the farm.

Judah expresses his gratitude for the sacrifice his father is willing to make for him but tells him that there will be no need for him to make the sacrifices. Judah has an idea on how he could, in this instance, create money. It is amazing how his financial knowledge comes into play when it's needed the most. It's apparent that wisdom is within Judah's grasp after all. Not all debt is bad debt and he has a hint on how he might just pull off this deal the smart way. It is perhaps time for him to benefit from using debt in an intelligent way. Using the strategy used by the banks, with people's money, Judah's plan will not only give him hectares of land, but was most likely to place him in a favorable financial position, for the years to ahead.

Judah still could not understand his father's change of heart so he asks him why he was doing all this. His father does not beat about the bush leveling it with him.

"I know that you will succeed because you have connected with your gift Son. If you had listened to me at one point, you would have missed it. Unfortunately, I missed it in thinking you were being stubborn, but now I know better. I was afraid to wean you off to the path of destiny. At times you pay a high price to walk that path, but after living a lifetime like I have done, you realize that if you don't walk it, you will never be truly satisfied in life. While we were your age, most of us watched Mr. Zebulun walk along that path, while we chose to do what was safe in our eyes and acceptable to those around us. As a result of his courage, Chris has now managed to achieve what most of us, will never achieve. As for me, I will be content knowing that I made a difference in my children's lives. If I am able to place each one of you at the center of your destinies then I will call myself successful. I played it safe all my life but now I am willing to risk everything to give you a chance to become all God intended you to be".

Judah could not help it but embrace his father. He held him for the longest time. It was not every father who put wind in his son's sail, like his father had just done.

"I love you Dad,"

"I'm proud of you Son!"

The words rang into his ears, to his very heart. His father had finally told him that he was proud of him. Those words would forever be a song on his heart. Knowing his father was proud of him, was the greatest gift his father had given him, and was ever going to give him. It meant the world to him and he was going to cherish this moment for the rest of his life.

Judah's financial acumen paid off and within a month the deal was completed. It was time for Judah to take a step that was going to make the gift within him, blossom like never imagined.

Chapter Twenty

The secret that's no secret at all

He knew just how to celebrate other people's victories and that is just what he did. Abba-Chris not only celebrated Judah's victory but he also expressed admiration for Judah's father. It was on this particular day that Judah finally came to know the secret behind Abba-Chris's success.

Judah told Abba-Chris everything and at the end, Abba-Chris clapped his hands, giving all glory to God. He glorified God for Judah's success as if he had been waiting expectantly and patiently for it.

It was then that Abba-Chris revealed to Judah that he was just an ordinary man who relied and depended on someone much bigger than him. Everything he was and had become was because he had connected himself to the source of it all. He was rich and his riches were just a portion of his blessings because he never forgot the source. He was a wealthy man, not only materially or financially but in everything.

He had amazing relationships with people. He had a beautiful marriage even though it was not immune to the challenges of marriage. Through conscious decision, each day he made himself fall in love with his wife all over again. His children were blessed, prospering and a blessing.

He was in excellent health not by chance but intentionally. He gave lavishly and still had more than enough, for whoever came to him. He was a rich man. Judah wanted to know his secret and Abba-Chris was now ready to share with him the secret of his life, which was really, no secret at all.

"You see Judah, when I was a young boy I heed a voice that said, *'follow me'*, and I started following. I have followed that voice since then and I will follow it for the rest of my life. When I heard about Jesus, I chose Jesus and despite what people said, I believed that *He is the Way, the Truth and the Life"* and I acted on the truth that I had heard. I chose Jesus, because we all want to know the way, and He is the way. We all want to know the truth, and He is the truth. We all want life, and He is the Life. I chose Jesus and I found it all in Him and honestly speaking I found more than I wanted or imagined possible".

"Son," he continues, "I made up my mind long back that there would be no turning back. If ever it had been told me that there is no heaven, that there is no God, I would still believe and hold onto Jesus. I have a bible I have read ever since that time and each time I read it, the teacher teaches me new things and I do them and I become. Hidden in the scriptures are the keys to life and God gladly reveals them to all his children, through the person of the Holy Spirit. The Holy Spirit is more than a teacher to me, Son. He is everything to me and I have grown to know Him better over the years. He is actually the One who has made me become who I am today, apart from Him I am nothing. But it all started with that one choice, choosing Jesus. That is my secret, Son, I chose Jesus Christ and I became complete in Him and He in me, Christ the hope of glory."

Abba-Chris's testimony literally causes Judah to feel an invisible set of arms wrapping around him. It's the presence of God which he is not familiar with. He feels the warmth and the acceptance. It feels so right to be where he is and it mellows his heart. It is like putting the puzzle of his life together and every piece finding its perfect connection. As he rests in that warmth, Judah reaches out to the God his mother had known and loved.

With eyes closed he quietly says, "Abba-Chris." Each of the following words comes from his innermost being, "Abba-Chris, I want to choose Jesus too".

"Go ahead, Son. It will be the best choice you will ever make in life".

So with that assurance Judah chooses Jesus to be his Lord and Saviour.

Judah was reconciled to God Almighty and it all made sense. Judah now understood why his mother always had a song of praise on her lips. He is truly God who puts a song in the heart of man. It now made sense to him, why his mother was always reading the bible and referring to it as the road-map to life.

What Judah was to learn in the days and years ahead of him, was that Jesus, was more than Lord and Saviour. He is everything and he was still to learn also that in *Christ Jesus everything consists9*.

As for Jeff, Judah was to learn that Jeff was his assignment. Just as he was Abba-Chris's disciple, Jeff was to be his disciple, but only when Jeff was ready to become all God intended him to become.

Jeff was a good guy who had built up walls all around him due to past hurt. It was not up Judah to change Jeff, but Judah determined in his heart to bring Jeff to a place where he would want change for himself. He promised himself that he was not going to give up on Jeff. Now that he knew, what he knew, he realized that as Abba-Chris had carried him in prayer to be where he is, and he too would pray for Jeff.

Judah was convinced that he could help Jeff and bring Jeff to realize that his gift was not inferior. Abba-Chris had told Judah that Jeff despised his gift, because he had not tapped into it in such a way that it could put food on his table. Jeff needed his eyes opened to the wealth that he carried inside himself. Judah's eyes were opened. His eyes of understanding were opened to the truth, opened to see the forest in the seed. Whenever he saw seeds he began to see the bigger picture of what was inside the seed, rather than just see the small dry seed.

There was so much he wanted to understand, but Abba-Chris never gave him more that he could chew at any given time. Learning was a process but at the end it attained its goal. Judah wanted to know why, if Jesus Christ was the answer to life, why so many people lived such miserable lives without hope. He wanted to know why so many people went through life without ever tapping into their potential. He wanted to know why the seed was camouflaged in such a way that only a few made use of it. Abba-Chris, being a wise teacher he was, encouraged Judah to turn to the bible for answers. He gave him the assurance that if he was prepared to learn, then the Holy Spirit would surely guide him to all truth.

Never had he imagined that a packet of spinach seeds would bring him onto the path of his destiny, but it had done just that. It was not really the packet of spinach seeds but rather God who had orchestrated everything, in response to the prayers his mother had made while she was still alive. God is no man's debtor. His mother had faithfully prayed that his son would one day know that his life is a seed waiting to be planted. Had Judah not responded in the way he did, and taken action, he would have missed his opportunity and God would not have saved him against his will.

Chapter Twenty-One

It's inside all

It had been a long day for him. Judah is dozing off to sleep as he is sitting. He mumbles something, "He put it in each and every one of us".

Abba-Chris looks at his wife, shares a smile and responds, "Yes Son, there is a gift within each and every one of us".

Abba-Chris smiles reflectively and mutters again, this time to himself, "Yes, the gift is within each and every one of us".

Prayer of Salvation

John 3: 16
For God so loved the world that He gave his only Son that whoever believes in him should not perish but have eternal life.

The invitation to have a genuine relationship with the Lord Jesus Christ is for whoever. If you have not yet made that decision to have a personal relationship with Jesus, you have an opportunity to do so.

Jesus loves you and He loves you very much.
Jesus Christ is the answer to all human problems and it's only when you have this relationship with Jesus Christ that you live life as God always planned it for you.

If you do not yet have a personal relationship with Jesus Christ and you want to have one with him, say this prayer with me:

O LORD God, I believe with all my heart that Jesus Christ is the Son of God.
I believe he died for me and God raised him from the dead. I believe He is alive today.
I confess with my mouth that Jesus Christ is the Lord of my life from today.
Through him and in his name I have eternal life. I am born again.
Thank you Lord, for saving me
I am now a child of God. Hallelujah

Congratulations

Now that you are born again:

i.   Realize you are now a new creature (literally) with no past – all things have become new 2 Corinthians 5:17

ii.   Start feeding your spirit daily with the Word of God – Joshua 1:8

iii.   Find a good bible-based church ad fellowship with the family of God. You are now a member of His body – the church

iv.   Share the good news of your salvation with others in your world and finally

v.   Live your life to the full- it is for this that Jesus came – so that you may have life and have it to the full John 10:10

God bless you

About the Author

Debbie Gumede (nee Gano) is a passionate prolific writer, pastor, teacher and public speaker whose greatest desire in life is to see people fulfill their destiny in life.

Her passion for writing started in her teenage years and has developed over the years. She is the founder of IKWIA (I Know Who I Am) Ministry, a ministry that focuses on underprivileged children and youth helping them find their true identity in Christ Jesus.

Contact details: debbiegumede9@gmail.com or +27 78 477 6393